MY NEXT BAD DECISION

New and Selected Poems: 1999-2014

To Dave & Ianka —

Enjoy!

MY NEXT BAD DECISION
New and Selected Poems: 1999-2014

by Nathan Graziano

artistically declined press
o r e g o n

First Edition
Published by Artistically Declined Press

Copyright 2014 Nathan Graziano
All rights reserved, including rights of reproduction in any form.

Cover & Interior Design by Ryan W. Bradley

ISBN 978-1-4951-1123-5
Artistically Declined Press
artisticallydeclined@gmail.com
www.artisticallydeclined.net

for Becky and Dr. Crocker

"It sounds insane
but it feels so right.
Your incremental suicide
is all that keeps you alive."

—Dan Cray, "Home Remedy"

INTRODUCTION
by Rebecca Schumedja

Nathan Graziano has always been daring with the subject matter that he selects, revealing an honest account of the trial and tribulations of humanity.

In *My Next Bad Decision*, the reader gets a complete picture of the unnamed first-person speaker and how he has navigated through life. We witness how the speaker who once "kissed an ugly girl and told her lies so she would like him" ends up a "Married Man Living in a Cheap Motel" where "There's a bottle of decent whiskey/on top of the mini-fridge, and a picture of his kids/smiling in the springtime sun on a nightstand beside his head." The confessions reveal the heroic side of vulnerability, how a man can easily sink into bad decisions no matter how much he wants to save himself and his family.

Regret is often expressed while in the midst of making mistakes, as seen in the poem "Apologies":

It's not premature for me
to apologize for this drink.
Or the one I'll pour next.

Your father can't see clearly
enough to drive you to the zoo
where the elephants remember
a young man with an arm
around his pregnant wife.

The speaker, fully aware of the pain he is causing, can't seem to change his behaviors, going as far as asking for forgiveness for a crime he has not yet committed. The desire to fix what has been broken is whispered throughout, but there is obvious tension between what the speaker wants and the decisions he makes. Graziano highlights this conflict in the poem "Useless with Tools:

The toolbox my father bought for me

a year after I moved into my own house
now sits in the basement beside the boxes
of my books that never sold and the publisher
shipped to me when he quit the business.

While the speaker possesses what he needs to fix the problem, he abandons hope in the basement alongside other unreached dreams.

At times, the speaker's lackadaisical attempts are infuriating to the reader, who witnesses the snowballing of his "bad decisions" and how they influence his family. Graziano creates a speaker who is an anti-hero and difficult to cheer on, but in the same way dynamic and irresistible. Just when you want to give up on him, the speaker shows you he is capable of love as seen in "A Few More Blankets Might Do:"

I remember when you were pregnant with our daughter,
we rented a slum apartment where the pipes
kept freezing in February, and we piled blankets
on top of our bodies, shivering, a chorus of teeth.

Graziano has an uncanny way of portraying relationships and how they change over time, as well as how they remain the same. Is the "Paper Ark" that the speaker built before his first wedding anniversary an admission of guilt? Does he use his imagination to a fault, building a paper ark that he insists will rescue his family from a turbulent world? Later, as his negative behaviors escalate, the "Paper Ark" becomes a "Tin Ship":

I watch our tin ship sink to the sand on the sea floor
as my last breath for us bubbles to the surface and explodes—
a sad mist then it's gone. Now you're alone, huddled on a rock,
a wry frown and your hair dripping down your pale back.
You've been here before; you know these stones and the starfish
by name, and the sky is the same sky you and I once lunged for
then died trying to save our tin ship, taking on water. Once,
my love, we had an ark made of paper that no one could sink.

Graziano bails the mistakes out of a sinking marriage and tosses them on the page. He reminds us that young love is often flooded by self-doubt and self-loathing, that sometimes the hero and the villain are inseparable. Graziano's ability to create multidimensional characters who are not afraid to offend sets him apart from other writers.

My Next Bad Decision shows how the transition from young adult to parent is anything but neat and that is what makes these poems engaging. We, as readers, can read about transgressions that we have committed but don't have the guts to share.

PART I:
THE LOST CAUSE

The Lost Cause

I was twenty-three years old and driving cross-country, alone,
cruising through Georgia in a red Honda with Rhode Island plates,
the windows rolled and my hand out, batting the breeze.

It was August, and sweat soaked through my tie dye Dead shirt.
I had a one-hitter on the dashboard and a low-dose of invincibility
as the windshield stiff-armed the Southern sun. In cheap sunglasses

I sung along with the sad songs on a break-up mix tape, mourning
the death of my car's air conditioning in the New Mexico desert.
However, with my whole life ready to unroll, I never mourned

for anything longer than a guitar solo. Stoned and smooth
and light, I pulled into a rest stop at midday and karate-chopped
the humidity as I got out of the car. I pissed in the restroom

beside a fat man with a red beard in a polo shirt, the collar popped.
He had the smugness of someone of neat business and filthy sex,
and I caught him glancing at my cock, groaning. I zipped up quick.

Back at my car, the doors locked and windows now rolled tight,
I spotted my keys sitting like a severed foot on the driver's seat.
Before cell phones, I was two-thousand miles from home—

meaning my parents' house. And in that Southern heat,
in a hostile land for Yankees, I tossed up my hands and kissed
my kid-buzz goodbye. I sat in the grass and cried like a beat-up boy.

The Drunkest I've Ever Been

My friends left me slumped in front
of a slot machine in Deadwood.
Two wilted cherries and a lemon
stilled in the dead eyes of fortune,
leaving me nothing but orange lint
in the sad linings of my jeans.

I hitched a ride in a pick-up truck,
curled in a fetal ball in back,
my coat pulled over my face
as the South Dakota winter
slapped me like a raw steak
on the bitter ride to my motel.

They tell me I kissed an ugly girl
and told her lies so she would like me.

When I Was Hamlet

Tonight I lay newly naked.
The old suit I used to wear
to weddings and funerals
hangs in the closet; its sleeves
dusty, gossamer on the lapels.

At one time, I charged my enemies,
raising a bottle-shaped sword.
Now I'm too fat for my old armor.
It's easier to close my eyes at night
and ignore the ghosts on the rooftop.

Sometimes It's Patsy Cline

She slow-danced in a hotel bar
in Boulder City, her hands on
the shoulders of a barrel-chested
hillbilly missing his two front teeth—
casualties from a sucker shot
in a honky-tonk brawl in Biloxi.

The jukebox whined with Patsy Cline;
whiskey tears dripped into a chipped
shot glass. Three cowboys wiped
their eyes dry with their bottlenecks.

She spoke to me with her lashes,
her head turned on the hillbilly's chest
as the song ended with the echo
of a steel guitar blowing in my ear.

The hillbilly bought us the next round
as she sat next to me and smiled.
Our fingers touched beneath the table
as we tapped two-step rhythms
with restless feet on a sawdust floor.

Morning

I woke before you
and waited for your eyes
to open, your hair
in tangles on the pillow,
your make-up washed off
in the bathroom sink.

You looked at me, scared
to be caught in the morning.

I got up to make you eggs.

Sweat

We stayed in bed
until the late afternoon,
the box fan pointed
at our bare backs.

The neighbor outside,
taking a break
from mowing his lawn,
told his wife,

"It's not the heat
but the humidity."
I lay on my stomach,
the breeze on my cheek.

I thought of getting up
but instead I watched
a single bead of sweat
trickle between your blades

then disappear in the curved
basin of your back. I tried
to catch it with my fingertips
but snared the air instead.

Say My Name

I've never asked someone to say my name
while having sex, although it doesn't seem too audacious

to ask your lover to say it, or scream it—unless,
your lover has a voice box or a stutter. Or a lisp,

the kind of speech impediment where they were removed
from class in grade school, and the speech therapist

showed up holding a file and smiling, all crooked teeth,
and, as polite as a hymn book, asked the person who would one day

become your lover to come—no dumb pun intended—
with them. Then your future lover would sit in a book closet

and practice saying their S sounds, saying "Sally sells seashells,"
although Sally isn't your name, of course. It's just practice.

Your name is Sisyphus— no relation to guy with the rock—
and after an initial bout of reticence and contemplations,

you finally asked your lover to say your name, mid-orgasm,
and your lover felt small and stupid and tongue-tied again

so now you'll never ask them to say your name during sex,
unless it slips out, and coitus comes to an embarrassing halt.

If I were ever to ask my own lover to "say my name"
while I was handcuffed to the bed frame, squirming in pain,

I'd be afraid she'd have a megaphone beneath the pillow
and say the name of the man she was thinking about,

or the name of the man I was pretending to be; mid-thrust,
she'd emasculate me, screaming, "Don't stop, Sisyphus!"

The Ants

She screamed from the other room. She had spotted an ant crawling across the kitchen floor in our apartment.

I stopped the letter I was writing to a friend and told her that there was little I could do about the ant in our apartment—other than step on the ant. I told her the ant had right to survey the kitchen floor in search of crumbs, and as long as the ant was willing to risk getting crushed under the weight of our shoes, we should commend the ant's bravery.

She didn't find this funny, nor would she kill the ant herself. "It's cruel," she told me. "Murder should be your job!"

I told her that I was unwilling to kill the ant. I told her that it wasn't my war. I heard her sigh from the other room.

Ten minutes later, she screamed again. She found another ant crawling in the cupboard.

Living on Grove St.

I.

"It is quiet here, and the neighbors
are respectable people," says the landlady
when she shows up at our front door
to warn us about making noise after ten p.m.

I tell her that the voices in my head
scream after midnight and there is not
a goddamn thing I can do to stop them.

She warns me about taking the Lord's name
in vain. "Blasphemy," she says. She says
she has lived here for forty years and three
generations of the sleepy cats who roam
the bushes, quietly. Silence is expected.

II.

Our neighbors vote straight Republican ballots.
Their parents vote straight Republican ballots.
Everyone on Grove St. votes straight Republican ballots
except for the Asian family who moved into the house
on the corner, but they're "just Asians, probably
China-lovers," the neighbors say. "But they're quiet."

I vote for the other guys, and last Tuesday evening
I went outside to retrieve the garbage cans wearing
a faded Grateful Dead t-shirt and sandals.

Word got out on Grove St. that the noisy couple
living 21A are also hippie communist liberals.

III.

On the good nights, we don't hear anything, no murmurs
from the neighbors or visits from our landlady.
Still, we make sure to pull the shades and burn incense
before smoking a joint and making slow love
on sheets filthy with whispered sex-talk.

Some nights, we hear country music and popping cans,
the hoots and hollers that follow the racecars
on a distant flat screen television. These are the nights
when we don't smoke pot. We listen to our music
softly and don't make sounds louder than mice in an attic.

IV.

The landlady shows up again, holding up two fingers.
"This is your final warning," she says. "If you want
to make noise, go back to where you came from.
Grove St. is a quiet place. Silence is expected here."
She lifts a poorly-penciled eyebrow, her hands resting
on her hips. I close the screen door and say,
"We'll consider it if you flash me a smile."

"One more complaint," she says, her make-up melting
into a puddles on her cheeks, her voice dying in the thick air.

V.

Word got out on Grove St. that the hippie communist
also writes poetry, according to the mailman—also votes
a straight Republican ballot—who saw suspicious envelopes.
It also came out that his girlfriend comes from California,
and the neighbors think she is a smokescreen. Everyone knows
there are a ton gays in California, and the neighbors suspect
the hippie cocksucker poet is one of those California fags.

"Did you see those limp wrists when he carries in
the garbage cans?" the neighbors says. "I don't know
what's worse: the gooks on the corner or the fag in 21A.
One thing is for sure: Grove St. is going to Hell."

VI.

The neighbors downstairs are related to the landlady;
it goes without saying, their rules are negotiable—
a perk for being respectable people. Some nights
they stay up late, and we're free to fuck to like blasphemers.

On the best nights, we sit up in bed and listen
to the neighbors' snores slide up the heating pipes.
I remind you that sound and smoke rise, and I reach
into the nightstand for a joint. We smoke quietly
and laugh at the noisy snores carrying up the pipes.

Looking at our neighbors, you can tell that they snore;
they choke on hot nights. I stand up and walk naked
to the bedroom window. The streetlights burn like matches
then Grove St. goes black. All us Asians, gays, blasphemers,
and the respectable people waiting for the sound of sunlight.

One Romantic

She is sitting on the stained couch
with the phone bill in her lap,
a plastic pen tucked behind her ear
and a simple calculator in her hand.
She twirls a strand of brown hair
around her index finger and sighs
and divides a large number by two.

I'm sitting cross-legged on the rug,
zoning out and picking at the blue carpet.
I'm thinking about how crisp the air
tastes in a bumpkin place like Kansas.

A Stranger Sleeps Next to Me

The electricity in our fights short-circuited months ago, and we are too tired to change the fuse. We shout at each other then our tongues turn to ashes, we blow smog, back and forth. The bed is the coldest place in the apartment. You come home from the bars, and I lie back on the pillow and pretend my throat is slit and I am dead. We make love, and I whisper that you are fucking a corpse. Drunk, you tell me you only want to get off. I watch a set of headlights splash the shadow of your jewelry box on the carpet. A stranger sleeps next to me—our backs to each other. The wall clock in the kitchen clamors in the silence of an apartment too small for two.

No White Horses

A tearful separation never fit either or us.

You sat on the edge of the bed, having flashes

of the same scene in a lifetime before me.

I spoke to you, smoking on a burning pulpit,

reaching into a tank full of rattlesnakes.

Your brown eyes, a pendulum, swung from me

to the wall to me to the wall. Our words

no longer belonged to us: they belonged to

a strong-jawed man in a black-and-white movie,

and a dark-haired beauty whose full lips

could only be crimson and courting a kiss.

My stomach sunk when I shut our bedroom door.

No white horses waited for me in the driveway

only my old red Honda as sirens screamed

somewhere in the city, and all the bars were closed.

Closing Wounds

I threw away the tear-soaked pillow
with my face's wasted indentation.

I made amends with my mattress
for flailing fists at it for five months.

I wrote our last love poem and buried
my last hope, six-feet deep, seeped in regret.

I wear you now only in my eyes
when someone mentions your name.

Seasonal Affective Disorder

One day the snow washes the color
from everything that matters.
The neighbor's skinny white cat
moves through shoveled paths,

unnoticed; I lock and bolt the door
to the second floor apartment
and listen to the wind pound
the old windows as I shiver.

The refrigerator is as empty
as the spaces between deep sleeps,
and I've forgotten what
an appetite tastes like anyway.

I remember a girl who laughed
while telling me a secret.
I remember her warm breath
on my neck, no color in her lips.

Comfortable Amnesia

I drive home with the radio off, the rain keeping time on the hood. Stopped at a traffic light, I glance in the rearview mirror at the line of white cars behind me, their tires low on air. Bloated and petulant faces stare at the red light, waiting to get home to someone who keeps their picture in a frame. I think about you. That's how it happens these days: you enter my mind for a second then you're replaced with an easier thought. The light turns green, and I drive forward into the rain, into the afternoon, into some place where it's safe to forget.

Corrina

Corrina. She holds the cocktail tray,
a brown torch, above her head,
never spilling a drop of drink
as she glides through the bar.
I learned her name from a receipt
a customer had left on a table.
Corrina. I say it to feel the syllables
roll off my tongue, a soft wave.
I let the undertow of inhalation
pull the vowels back inside
my mouth, and I say it again.
Corrina. I smile when she walks by,
leaving a faint scent of French fries.
I say her name to myself. Corrina.
My voice drowned by the jukebox.

Tough Odds

I used to live in Vegas
where I learned a little
something about odds.
One night when you
caught me looking at you,
I was trying to calculate
my odds of ever tucking
a strand of blond hair
behind your delicate ear—

the odds were the same
as a sandcastle falling
in love with rain.

And With This Being Said

The gray skies are so thick
bright thoughts suffocate.

At this desk, in monastic silence,
I wait for you to arrive.

We won't do anything extraordinary,
sit on the couch and sip drinks;

we will watch the night pass
with the patience of priests.

And with that being said,
I'll fold my hands and wait for you.

The Ghost of an Ex-Girlfriend

I swear I saw her pumping gas, standing
beside the silver hatchback she drove.
I caught a glimpse of her profile
and when I tried to look closer—gone.

Another time she was a shadowy figure
in the corner of a Greek restaurant,
staring a me through a martini glass
then disappearing behind a menu.

Once she was sitting at a bus station
with a blue duffle bag by her feet.
But I only saw the back of her head
before the Greyhound swallowed her.

I doubt that I'm the only one who sees
the ghost of his ex-girlfriend.
I doubt that I'm the only one who hears
her soft sobs when a room gets quiet.

I Knew You'd Be My Wife

We found shelter in an old Western saloon,
waiting out a flash flood in Cheyenne.
Thunder crashed as five feckless faces
watched us from wooden stools,
sipping from their bottled beers.

The pop country music played,
a toothache on the jukebox.
We ordered pitchers of Bud Light
from a waitress in cut-off jean shorts
and sipped our beers with no place to be.

I decided then I'd ask you to marry me
as the storm passed and I glanced at your glass
jealous of the lipstick smeared on its rim.

PART II:
HONEY, I'M HOME

Remembering Our First Apartment

Julia, the fat woman without a job
who lived in the apartment beside us,
stood on the top step of her front porch
with a cigarette dangling from her lips,
she shouted out the side of her mouth
at Dorothy, the fat woman without a job
who lived in the apartment above us.
Julia told Dorothy to "get off [her] fat ass
and move [her] shitbox car" so she could
"get out of the fucking driveway and go
to the goddamned liquor store before it closes."
Dorothy then called Julia a "skanky-ass fat ho"
and told her to "come off the porch
and say that shit to [her] fucking face."
Julia flicked her cigarette at Dorothy
and started to waddle off the porch saying,
"You just fucking try that shit, bitch-slut."
Then Max, Julia's meth-smoking boyfriend,
burst out onto the front porch in his briefs
and told Julia to "shut [her] goddamn pie-hole
and get the fuck inside. [He has] to work at 5 a.m."

My wife, watching it from the bedroom window,
nudged me and said, "Pay attention, honey.
Someday you'll write a poem about this."

Lily White Noon

My wife wrote "lily white noon"
on the cover of a woman's magazine
scribbled beside a blue ink heart.

These words are a riddle I can't solve.
If they're random, why did she choose
these three words from a plentiful list?
Why not something more exotic
like "sultry platinum eucalyptus"?

Maybe she was on the telephone,
a pen in her hand, listening to her sister
share plans to elope with her boyfriend
at a chapel in a small New Hampshire town.

Or maybe my wife, staring out
the kitchen window of our first house,
gave up trying to describe the sunlight
and how it glazed the grass in a way
that her words failed to capture.

The Inevitable Surprise

"Good God, he has a baseball bat between his legs," my wife says and covers her mouth, trying to blot the grin that slipped on her lips as the pizza boy flipped the lid of a pepperoni pie and presented a wide-eyed bombshell with what Edgar Allan Poe called "the inevitable surprise." I say, "No, no," the air siphoned from my Friday night, "the camera adds six inches." But my wife knows. And I know. And anyone who has watched *Pizza Bone 6* and seen the look of sheer fear in the bombshell's eyes when that lid was flipped—yes, you know, too. So I turn to my wife and suggest some popcorn and a new movie, one where the hero dies at the end.

Red Car Girl

I.

The red car stops in the driveway
across the street.
The engine cuts and dies.

I am a specter evanescing
behind the storm door
I never replaced with a mesh screen
for the spring, and now
we swelter in August's closed fist.

She steps out of the red car
in a pair of cut-off jeans
and a pink tank top.
Two strands of black hair
spill from a ponytail.
She flips them off her face
and transfers her keys
from palm to palm to pocketbook.

My body holds its breath
as I stand there, graying,
a married man with his vows
loosely sown to his dry lips.

II.

My best friend in high school
snapped a photo of a cheerleader's ass
in skintight stonewash jeans.

She seemed to be posing, hip cocked
in the crowded halls by her locker,
her back to my friend—as always—

her long black hair licking
the small of her back.

My best friend printed copies,
and I kept the picture in a shoebox
filled with old baseball cards—
the players who were not my heroes.
Each night, I'd take out the picture.

The girl never knew my name,
and I never saw her face,
but I imagined us in love,
driving through town together.
I had one hand on the steering wheel
and the other lodged to her denim thigh.
We were a couple from a Springsteen song,
racked with savage suburban passion.

Afterwards, I'd place the picture back
in the shoebox beside a bench player
and cradle my pillow, pretending
I was holding my cheerleader, post-coital.

III.

Sometimes I imagine the Red Car Girl
sees me standing behind the storm door
and runs her tongue's smooth tip,
slow and sultry, over her top lip—
blood-red and glossed thick.

She crosses the street, her hips
swaying like a surrender flag
then she knocks on the storm door,
lightly with fists of felt.

From there it's all wild hands

and eyes and tongues moving
drunk over each other's flesh.

From there it's all hard cock
and swollen cunt pumping
in the white hot sex of summer.

Drenched in the sheets, she whispers,
"Turn me over and fuck me again.
Face your wedding picture, punk."

IV.

I was sixteen and scared the first time
I slept with a real woman.

Scared I'd come too quick.
Scared the condom would slip.
Scared of what I couldn't get back.
Scared my fantasies would be better.
Scared of the feral noises.
Scared her parents would come home.
Scared of cheap apartments and tiny feet.
Scared I'd have to pay half on an abortion.
Scared I'd have to get a job.
Scared she was faking her pleasure.

And she was.

V.

Sometimes the storm door is shattered
by my longings and imagined lusts,
so instead we fuck in the backseat
of the red car while a cat cries at midnight.

We steam the windows with hot gasps.

Too heated to undress, I pull her bra
over her breasts, and slip my cock out
the zipper of my loose blue jeans.
I slip her cut-off denim shorts off
those two long gulps of white leg
and slide her panties down to her ankles.
My mouth becomes a full moon as I say,

"I'm going to fuck you, Red Car Girl.
Fuck you. Fuck you. Deep."

VI.

My college girlfriend slept with me
the first night we met, the keg beer
pungent and fresh on our breath.

Isn't that something?

VII.

Sometimes I picture my wife
and The Red Car Girl tangled in tanned flesh,
breasts pressed to breasts, fingers
finding the spots a man will never know.
They lie in the uncut grass, Whitman-esque,
their flesh damp with morning dew.

My wife's hands are tangled in
black hair as The Red Car Girl licks her.
My wife's hips crack as she shouts
above the choir of birds and crickets,

"Why the hell did I marry that boy?"

VIII.

The Red Car Girl walks from her car
to her house, dripping sex and oblivious

of the storm door in the summertime,
the graying specter fading behind it,

of fantasies and poems that when written
will never come close
to a good old American fuck.

Happy Hour at The Dead Man's Saloon

I dream of The Dead Man's Saloon
where there's a gathering of ghosts
who usually reside on my bookshelves.

In the back, Dosteovsky sits stone-faced
in dark glasses at a card table,
palming an ace. He raises Mark Twain,
who folds as Faulkner spits chaw
on the sawdust floor and calls.

Meanwhile, belly-up at the bar,
sharing a bottle of expensive red wine,
Freud and Sophocles snicker
at the fact that my wife and my mother
share the exact same name.

My Daughter's Eyes

The final slices
of afternoon sun
strain through chinks
in the blinds
into the bedroom
where I watch
my daughter sleep
while listening
to the Red Sox game
on the clock radio.
For the first time
I understood
what people mean
when they say
she looks like me.

It's mostly in the eyes.

I look closer,
and sure enough,
see myself at a time
before things
made me ugly.

Western Binge

I'm a washed-up star from a Western movie,
saddled to this old oak kitchen stool,
watching my youth play back in film reels,
slicing each time the lights go on or the baby cries.

My wife lies awake in her dressing-room bed,
tossing in the sheets where I'm not sleeping.
There are things inside me right now
that want to go in the bedroom, hat in hand,
touch my lips to her forehead and tell her:
"I love you. I'm sorry." To lay down my gun.

But the words are rabbit bones stuck in my throat;
I can't choke them down with the house whiskey.

My daughter crawls across the sawdust floor.
After each small jaunt forward, she falls
flat on her gut. Then the little cowgirl gets up.

Paper Ark

I.

It seems appropriate
nine days before
our first anniversary
cold water would leak
from the ceiling
in our basement.

A problem we cannot
afford to fix.

So we set a mop bucket
below the drip

and watch
and wiggle
our wedding rings.

Water logged,
I build an ark
our of old newspaper.

In case of a flood.

II.

We never had a real wedding,
according to the rules
of real wedding people.

There are supposed
to be invitations
printed in calligraphy,
banquet halls

and plated chicken dinners,
open bars and drunken uncles
and peach chiffon
bridesmaids' dresses.

There is supposed
to be a bridal gown
white like a new thought,
lacy with a train
and a veil to hide
anxious eyes.

There is supposed to be
a wedding song
and a slow dance.

It's never supposed to rain.

III.

The bucket is about to overflow.
But we bought this house
knowing I couldn't fix a leak.

I don't own a toolbox.

You're pacing
the kitchen floor
on the phone
with your father.
He tells you to find a man
who can confront pipes
and save you from the drip
that spits on your security.

He tells you
that a poet in a leaky house

is like an atheist in a foxhole.
It's the only simile he knows.

He might be right.

But he hasn't seen my ark.

IV.

Some nights we wish
for more bed between us.
Our tirades turn into sighs
that turn into snores, eventually.

Some nights we can't sleep
in the same bed
so one of us carries
a blanket and pillow to the couch
and slips into a restless slumber
in front of the blue glow
of the television set.

Some nights the baby
sleeps between us.
We reach for each other's hands
and apologize with our fingertips.

V.

The three of us board
the paper ark I built
while the world drowns
in the things we can't afford.

I sing sailor songs
and hold you both

while we dance to the rhythm
of a distant basement drip.

A slow dance.

Our wedding song.

Useless with Tools

I concede that I can't fix the bathroom floor,
or seal the back door, or implore you
to see my masculine deficiencies with mercy.

The toolbox my father bought for me
a year after we moved into this house
now sits in the basement beside the boxes
of my books that never sold and the publisher
shipped to me when he quit the business.

The books in the boxes jeer at me so I avoid
the basement and its bevy of bad behaviors.

There is a coup being planned to behead me,
I try to explain to my wife; the ratchet wrenches
joined the drill bits, and the hammer is immersed
in *Mein Kampf* while I hide beneath the bed.

The walls are crumbling in this home I own;
there's a toolbox in the basement, fully equipped,
but my dumb ass couldn't drill a board.

The Onset of Dark

The Christmas tree is bagged in plastic,
a corpse tossed beside the curb;
its stiff needles splayed in dirt and snow.

The eggnog in the fridge has spoiled
beside six headless gingerbread men,
one pardoned by the dog on New Year's Day.

I could walk to the nearest liquor store
with my eyes closed, sniffing out the patches
of black ice that threaten to snap my neck.

Listening to "Desolation Row"
in Back of Jim's Car on the Way to Bar in Buffalo

Again, I'm tangled in my own uncut hair, too drunk to dice the differences between "desolation" and "decision." They might be homonyms.

Outside a convenience store, a man has been shot; a Samaritan's coat covers his torso. The shot man's legs twitch and his feet kick as the ambulance approaches in a holy glow of red light.

Jim describes the place we're going to as "ironically seedy," a cesspool of hipsters. "The artistes stand at the bar and pose like basement mannequins," he says. Jim is a painter; I'm a poet. What are we doing? We need to make a decision on desolation, whether it is worth it or not.

Bob Dylan sold out, eventually.

A man is dying, his head resting on a curb.

I can't stop drinking.

Apologies

Your toys are scattered—
singular building blocks,
a stuffed puppy without tags.

But I've made the mess.

Your four-toothed smile
lingers in my absence,
in a place where you're safe
with your mother.

It's not premature for me
to apologize for this drink.
Or the one I'll pour next.

Your father can't see clearly
enough to drive you to the zoo
where the elephants remember
a young man with an arm
around his pregnant wife.

Screwed by the Easter Bunny

My two year old son scrapes rabbit shit from his shoe
with a twig from a dying tree. He tells me,
"The Easter Bunny isn't coming this year."
No baskets, no eggs, no chocolate critters to behead.

"He's not coming," my son screams.

I tell him rabbits don't have thumbs;
therefore, they could never hold a basket
or palm an egg and keep plausibility intact.

Rabbits certainly don't have the giving instinct
or the desire to watch a loved one's eyes light up
like a pair of new suns rising behind a closed tomb.

Starting next year, I tell my son, we'll stop
celebrating rabbits and resurrections on Easter.
Instead, we'll toast the absence of ghosts
and the empty spaces beneath the kitchen sink.

And in place of painted eggs, we'll stuff our fists
in our mouths then joyride through cemeteries
listening to the static hum and sports' talk on AM radio.

Like a room of cynics, drunk at a séance,
we'll cry shenanigans as we shift the candle's flame
and scoff at the things we don't feel or see.

Bad Dad

I've failed to fit the big shoes.
From the tips of my toes
to the end of the soles,
there is space enough to build
a boy's bedroom and fill it with wishes.

My beard is not robust enough
to sop the tears you've spilled
skinning your knees, waiting for me
to heal you with a man's hug.

While drunk in my armchair,
you stand in the backyard,
the crabgrass growing like dreams
around your feet, holding a bat
and waiting for me to spill out
the door and toss the first soft pitch.

Maybe the Romans Just Got Old

I consider the cold beer in the fridge
and weigh it against the inevitable fall
of my bones, the toppling of this terror frame
whose flimsy pillars can no longer hold
the morning sun on its bloated roof.
And one beer won't stop at two or six.
There's years of momentum moving forward,
a sack of rocks flung toward two a.m.
when I'll crawl in bed beside my wife
and slur confessions to small-time crimes.

There's nothing new about a tired man
who sees tombstones each time he tries
to recover from another weekend drunk
and finds prescription pills spilled on his tongue.
He floats through those gray days
half-awake in a pharmaceutical haze.

Maybe Rome didn't collapse from greed
and the need to watch the world fall to its knees.
Maybe Bacchus just got old and failed to be
the god everyone once admired, observing
the orgies from the sidelines, a finger in his ear.
Then the Romans, seeing the god in sunglasses
with vomit on his sandals, threw up their hands
as it all went to hell with profound disappointment.

Summer Lightning

"It's going to be all right," I whisper without moving my lips.
Our kids are in bed between us while the thunder shrugs,

wrapped in black clouds as the sky's switch is fiddled.
The rain taps the window like a courteous burglar.

We lie as still as sculptures of our sleeping selves,
impenetrable beneath the sheet covering our legs.

Behind my eyes, my vices draw guns—sons of bitches.
They've pulled down the blinds, cordoned my mind.

They've shown havoc to you, me, and the precious lives
between us, whose tiny breath is as soft as a piano's tears.

Crash. Our son is startled awake. Brave boy—he pushes out
his bony chest, biting his lip and he says, "I'm all right,"

as our daughter buries herself in the nook of my arm
and seeks shelter and relief in the safety of my shoulder.

Now in my thirties, a husband and a father, I flex
to protect the three of you from the violence of the storm.

But with every roof I've built, my good intentions can't patch
the holes my vices stab with shards from broken bottles.

Here, in this summer storm, six days without a drop,
I gather you and our children in my still-shaking arms

then put my vices to rest, bully them to sleep
and promise—my family, my loves—"It's going to be all right."

PART III:
CONFESSIONS OF A RECOVERING CRIER

In Anticipation of My Next Bad Decision

Saturday afternoon sits like a bully on my head.
I crack another beer and watch college football,
those impossibly beautiful cheerleaders smiling

on the sidelines in those impossibly short skirts.
They're launched like bright thoughts in the sky
with sturdy young men ready to catch them

then they'll all crowd around the camera and wag
their index fingers—they're all Number One—
with Saturday night and nice lives ahead of them.

My therapist says I have a drinking problem
and calls it a form of insanity. He compares it
to a helium balloon I expect to stay grounded

without a string tying it to anything solid. He says
I should try to get some exercise in the winter
when I tend to be depressed, so tonight

I'm going to shadow box in the garage
by the light of a lamp my wife and I never used.
We bought it at a yard sale when we were broke

and eating pancakes for all three meals.
But I always had money for drinks, and I think
my therapist may have a point. It's something

I knew when I was in college and trying to plan
my next step up the stairs, but I'd stumble back down,
hitting the ground, with nobody there to catch me.

Men with Mustaches

A man with a mustache must be watched closely,
like a storm cloud concealing lighting in its coat.

A man with a mustache might be a porn star,
a scrawny guy with three legs, sweating pools of fuck.

A man with a mustache might sell you a used car
and promise it will change the way you drive. It will.

A man with a mustache might wear his shirt unbuttoned,
his chest hair screaming like a room full of pop-fans.

A man with a mustache might sell tickets
for The Ferris Wheel, piss behind the dunking booth.

A man with a mustache might try to write like Hemingway
but only succeed in drinking himself to sleep.

A man with a mustache might, in fact, be me
before I shaved it off after scaring myself in the mirror.

A man with a mustache must be watched closely:
I guarantee he's looking at you, chewing on a toothpick.

Three Scorpion Bowls

Scorpion Bowl #1: At the table beside us, a young couple sucks down their Scorpion Bowl through long red straws. It's May, and we're in a Japanese restaurant where Christmas Muzak pipes through the ceiling. My wife and I sip iced teas and try to keep our kids from impaling each other's eyes with chopsticks.

Scorpion Bowl #2: The young man moves closer to the young girl and rolls up his sleeve to show her his new tattoo. "It's symbolic of stuff," he says. The young girl tosses back her head and sings, "The weather outside is frightful, but the fire is so delightful," as my son plunges his hand in the seaweed salad. "Dragon boogers," he yells. I order another iced tea.

Scorpion Bowl #3: The young girl, her voice rising, says to the young man: "If I'm still able to walk after we finish drinking, I'll totally fuck you tonight." The young man lets the straw drop from his lips and reaches for his wallet. As our children are momentarily occupied with the exotic fish in a wall-sized tank, my wife nudges my shin with her foot. "Do you remember when we used to be like them?" she asks. After seven years, two kids and countless near-separations, I nod. "I'll totally fuck you tonight," I say and show her my tattoo.

Confessions of a Recovering Crier

For three years, not one tear has streamed
down my cheek, not one wet lash to wish on.

As a younger man with a thirst like baked dirt,
I would bawl over beers for hours, calling
friends at three a.m. during weeknight binges.

I'd sob into the phone: "I miss you, man,"
to my best friend Dan, drunk in Missouri.

"I've fucked up my life," I'd cry to my wife
while fixing, on ice, the evening's second nightcap.

One time in college, I fell from a barstool
and puked on my shoes as the patrons applauded.
Then the bouncer slapped a stone-heavy hand
on my slumped shoulder and snarled, "Leave."
I fell to my knees, and pleaded, and cried,
claiming I was framed by the bartender.

These days, I drink and cry less and some people
have asked if I'm off the sauce. "No way," I'll say,
"but I'm a recovering crier." And I'll point to my eyes
as dry as hide and swell with what some call pride.

The Waitress

The waitress' fingers touch mine
when she hands me the beer.
The waitress' feet brush my toes
when she brings my family their food.
The waitress and I exchange
helium brows and "fuck me" eyes.

Sucked into a cloud of fried-food,
we escape for fifteen minutes
and disappear to a motel movie set
I imagined one afternoon
when I was drunk and being half-honest.

She closes the cheap red velvet drapes
and offers me the last drag of the first smoke
from the pack she bought with her tips.
She tell me that she plans to get married.

She talks about my wife while slipping off
her sweater and stepping out of her skirt.
She mentions my book, the one that she read,
while unclasping her bra, and we balk
in the chokehold of stale smoke and cry.

The waitress knows me and my family,
serves us pizza and fills my beer
when it's low—not finished, but almost.

Waiting for the Cable Man

It's a catastrophe of Old Testament proportions,
Gomorrah is a vacation-getaway by comparison
to a house without the television's daily distortions.

The cat has been on a hunger strike since
this blight befell our house. No longer scared,
the mice shit in the kitchen, without consequence.

I watch for the cable man from the living room,
my breath halted and hands clenched in prayer,
waiting for the giver of light, the remover of gloom.

One Time You Called Me O.J.

"The glove doesn't fit," I said, my transgressions
stabbing into your shoulder blades.
Shame, dressed as a gardener, slipped out the back gate.

One time you called me O.J. so I called you a cunt
and, to this day, I swear when you glared back,
your eyes throwing knives, that look contained

the potential to kill. "The glove doesn't fit,"
I said as your hair slashed my hands
when you whipped around your head. "Bullshit," I said.

That was the first time you called me O.J.
There have been others. Like the time I lied
about where I'd been when I came home at two a.m.

and you reached for my throat in bed and grabbed
my second face instead. I shook my head.
"The glove doesn't fit. Bullshit," I said. "Bullshit."

But things were over by then. I had ruined them.
We had stopped being glamorous and walking
together at night, piercing our ears with stars.

The Athleticism of Gluttony

An Asian kid built like a cigarette
mows down hot dog after hot dog—
three bites, a machine-like rhythm.

His body metabolizes those pig's asses
and the white bread buns at a bionic pace
like a broken man through a shredder.

At what point, I wonder, did this kid
first hear his calling, a ghost's voice
whispering to him from a hot dog cart?

"Three bites," it called, and the boy obliged.
The camera pans on his proud parents,
sitting beside a sleeveless man in a mesh hat.

The husband reminds his wife, by touching
her hand, of the night they conceived him,
moonlight swallowing the stars without trying.

A Winter Evening at Supercuts

The gray hair fell from the electric clippers.
Outside, the snow-drifts threw errant fists,
bruising each other in the dark strip-mall lot,
moving fast past parked cars and floodlights
like an old man moves fast past a mirror.

I'm not bald but the other night, restless
at four a.m., I watched a Rogaine infomercial,
hoping to cure my insomnia, but instead
found myself cheering for the dog-faced guys
in their "before" pictures, before their midlife crises
crawled onto their hairlines and died.

The young woman cutting my hair apologized
for not offering me a shampoo first, whispering
with spearmint breath into my ear that her boss,
an older hairdresser with her glasses on a chain,
cited her for the same offense the previous week.
I told the young woman to clip the rest of my head
then I lied and told her that it was my birthday.

For My Sister, On Her Wedding Day

Take heed of the saints who sing among us.

Take heed of the saints who slow dance, ethereal,
among the delicate dust on the polished pews.

Take heed of The Saint who always said,
"Condemn the sin, but not the sinner."

Your strength, my sister, will always rest
in the easy way you smile, like a simple prayer,
while the house burns down around you.

Your strength, my sister, will always lie,
not in decibels of your yells, or the way you play
a mythical fiddle, but in the jokes you whisper
in your husband's ear as the flames flick your faces.

Becoming Anonymous

For two years, he slept beside stones,
hiding any accidental arousals
the mornings after he dreamed
of a woman's soft mouth pressed
against his own; driving home
from work, he could not stop
his car from pulling into the bar.
The wheels had minds and minded
the cold tar beside her car.

One night he never went home,
and his wife never noticed.
She thought he was walking the dog
through a boundless and snarling fog;
or he was picking up a name on his way
back from being anonymous for years.

The D Word

The fights extend like spools of a hangman's rope.
Weeks will pass without the crisp snap of a neck.

Each morning we meet at the bathroom door
as silent as mannequins with stretched necks.

In the kitchen, she'll stab the chicken breasts
as we bicker about a pot of boiling red potatoes.

Later, she'll turn her back in bed, and I'll leave
the room and doze on the couch, one eye open.

When the D word drops on our conversation
like a dead body falling from the hall closet,

we'll stand there and sigh and shield our eyes,
both praying away our prints on the twisted knife.

A Married Man Living in a Cheap Motel

The clothes hangers by the door are downward bent,
tortured from the weight of so-many car keys in suit coats
and dresses that women didn't want wrinkled.

The bedspread pukes its usual plant-and-floral patterns,
and the mattress' springs makes the floor seem forgiving.
I thought it might snow, but the sun smuggled its way

into mid-afternoon. There's a bottle of decent whiskey
on top of the mini-fridge, and a picture of my kids
smiling in the springtime sun on a nightstand beside my head.

For the first time in years, I took off my wedding ring,
pretended to flush it with a whiskey piss—my wife, the woman
I love, is only miles away, and she may be sobbing, too.

The Man Code

The Man Code says you can get drunk for her, once,
cry if your eyes are itchy, if your face needs hydration,
then buck up and fuck a stranger, find the loosest girl
in the bar and lead with your best line. You might try:
"Did it hurt, beautiful, when you fell from the sky?"
Whatever you do, when you get her back to your motel—
the one where you've been living for a week since your wife
asked you to leave, and it reeks of stale cigarette smoke
and Febreze, with a toilet that tilts ten degrees to the left—
be sure you put away the picture of your six-year old son,
the one you've kept on the nightstand, the one where your boy
is smiling and the space between his missing front teeth
seems big enough to drive through with a truck of apologies.
Once the girl is naked, and you're naked, and you're both
writhing beneath the bleached sheets, be sure not to say
that you miss your wife, be sure you don't whimper
and offer her the cab fare home. The Man Code says,
if you do, you're definitely a pussy, a homo, a human being.

Another Friday Night

At one time, on Friday nights, my thirst for your flesh
surged with every drink, my drunk begun and ended with you.
We sang songs on our porch, my guitar in need of new strings.

With slight hangovers the next morning, we'd take our kids
to a small breakfast diner by the hospital and wait in line
for fresh omelets and crisp bacon and endless coffee.

Tonight—Friday—I get drunk in a cheap motel, alone,
with the drone of a television tuned to the news.
I sip bourbon from a plastic cup and try not to cry.

With a hangover tomorrow morning, I'll meet you at noon
to pick up the kids and take them for pizza at a restaurant
where the waitresses know me and the beers pour forever.

A Tin Ship

I.

You asked me for the last life-preserver
and I told you I threw it overboard with the bottles,

all in an attempt to stay afloat, but we were taking
on water quicker than we could lift and bail.

In a tin ship, you vowed to sink with me, drown
like you knew how to drown—like we'd done it before—

then, as our lips met the cold tide, you smiled
and swam toward the lighthouse, an elegant backstroke.

II.

Only underwater, the air squeezed from one's veins, does one
understand the study of solitude, being one with nothing.

I watch our tin ship sink to the sand on the sea floor
as my last breath for us bubbles to the surface and explodes—

a sad mist then it's gone. Now you're alone, huddled on a rock,
a wry frown and your hair dripping down your pale back.

You've been here before; you know these stones and the starfish
by name, and the sky is the same sky you and I once lunged for

then died trying to save our tin ship, taking on water. Once,
my love, we had an ark made of paper that no one could sink.

The Cold Room Circus

I rented a single room on the second floor
of a townhouse: a cat's mouth clean and big-top bright
but so cold I would roast my sullen bones beside
a space heater I bought at a yard sale last summer.

My kids lived three miles from the cold room
in the warm house I owned with their mother,
the woman I called my wife for a decade
until one night I fell asleep with a lit cigarette

and the bed burned and left bitter cinders
beside ashes shaped like pointed fingers.
I saved my wedding ring from the fire and used it
to teach my pain to jump through flaming hoops.

I watched the circus of sadness while eating popcorn
beside the ghost of a man who once swallowed knives.
An air mattress sat on the floor of the cold room to catch
my loneliness, its hair on fire, walking the high wire.

A Few More Blankets Might Do

I placed the air mattress beside the window
and wake every half hour, shivering, teeth chattering,
trying to insulate myself with a few more blankets.
This room I rented with utilities included meant
I couldn't control the thermostat, my climate.

Shivering, I suppose this is a real-deal separation,
being apart until one of us hits a scratch ticket
and can afford a lawyer. I've placed my wedding ring
in front of the school pictures of our son and daughter,
smiling beneath hot lamps and studio backgrounds.

I remember when you were pregnant with our daughter,
we rented our first slum apartment where the pipes
kept freezing in February, and we piled blankets
on top of our bodies, shivering, a chorus of teeth.

Crash

It's a collision in slow motion.
Our kids are the casualties.

We smoke the cigarettes we quit
as a leaf pile blazes in the neighbor's yard.

I pluck the burning grass from our lawn
and offer it to a trail of smoke.

"I've never been more in love
than when we met," you whisper.

Wiping the blood from my brow, I agree.

ACKNOWLEDGEMENTS

Many of these poems originally appeared—some in radically different forms—in *Not So Profound*, which was published by the now-defunct Green Bean Press in 2002, and *After the Honeymoon*, published by Sunnyoutside Press in 2009.

Nothing was off-limits when choosing these poems, so some of these poems can be plucked from these now out-of-print chapbooks: *No White Horses* (GBP, 2000), *Seasons from the Second Floor* (GBP 2001) and *Honey, I'm Home* (Sunnyoutside Press, 2005).

"Red Car Girl" and "Paper Ark" originally appeared as broadsides from The Rooftop Series and Sunnyoutside Press, respectively.

Of course, I need to acknowledge the journals that originally published the new work in this collection, not that an acknowledgment is adequate payment for all the hard work the editors put into publishing these journals: *Nerve Cowboy, Thieves Jargon, My Favorite Bullet, The Meadow, Words Dance, The Fox Chase Review, Poiesis, Trachodon, Milk, Full of Crow, Clutching at Straws, Underground Voices, Red Fez, The Orange Room Review* and *The Chiron Review.*

Without Ryan W. Bradley, the publisher of Artistically Declined Press, taking on this project years ago, you wouldn't be reading this (if you are, in fact, reading this). I decided to abandon the chronological approach to my work and tried, instead, to string together a loose narrative with a fictional speaker through the poetry I've written in the past 15 years.

A special thanks to Becky Schumejda for writing the introduction and saving this manuscript.

Finally, much love, as always, goes to my wife, Liz. You've put up with twelve years of me writing this stuff, and we've somehow managed to stay married. Your support for me and my work has been invaluable. I love you.

Nathan Graziano lives in Manchester, New Hampshire. He is the author of three collections of poetry—*Not So Profound* (Green Bean Press, 2003), *Teaching Metaphors* (Sunnyoutside Press, 2007) and *After the Honeymoon* (Sunnyoutside Press, 2009)—a collection of short stories, *Frostbite* (GBP, 2002), and several chapbooks of fiction and poetry. A chapbook of short prose pieces titled *Hangover Breakfasts* was published by Bottle of Smoke Press in 2012, and Marginalia Publishing released a novella titled *Some Sort of Ugly* in 2013.

For more information, visit his website at www.nathangraziano.com.

CPSIA information can be obtained
at www.ICGtesting.com
Printed in the USA
FSOW01n0855081014
3211FS